VOLUME 77 OF THE YALE SERIES OF YOUNGER POETS

Icehouse Lights

DAVID WOJAHN, 1953 -

FOREWORD BY RICHARD HUGO

YALE UNIVERSITY PRESS, NEW HAVEN AND LONDON

Published with assistance from the
Mary Cady Tew Memorial Fund.

Designed by Sally Harris
and set in Galliard type by
Typographic Art, Inc., Hamden, Conn.
Printed in the United States of America by
Alpine Press, Stoughton, Mass.

Library of Congress Cataloging in Publication Data

Wojahn, David, 1953-
    Icehouse lights.

    (Volume 77 of the Yale series of younger poets)
    I. Title.   II. Series: Yale series of younger
poets; v. 77)
PS3573.044I23   811'.54   81-16018
ISBN 0-300-02816-4   AACR2
ISBN 0-300-02817-2 (pbk.)

10 9 8 7 6 5 4 3 2 1

I know,
I know and you know, we knew,
we did not know, we
were there, after all, and not there,
and at times when
only the void stood between us we got
all the way to each other.
                              —*Paul Celan*

Contents

Foreword

In "Distance," the first poem in this book, two men appear: a poet up late writing, and a workman from a building project across the street who stays after the shift is over. The poet types. The worker sings to himself and perhaps aimlessly or perhaps to beat time ". . . drums a hammer again / and again into the ground." Each hears the other, and that's important. The two men are parts of the same mind, one that must earn a living and one that must write poems. The quotidian self can but play to his own ear. He is the sole audience for his art. The poet comes

> . . . to admire
> the distance between us,
> the noises we make to ourselves
> in the night. . . .

So the poet recognizes that although they are separated by an admirable distance, they also have much in common. The workman cannot admit anything external or animal into his song; "The cats on the roof disturb him."

On the other hand, the poet can receive the unexpected and foreign and find in them a welcome simile. It is through the simile that both men, both selves, become united, become

> . . . tired
> as the lovers in a Japanese print,
> who've turned and wiped their genitals
> with the blue silk scarves
> they had stuffed in their mouths
> while coupling.

Poems would be easy to write if as poets we could discard that other self, that workman who sings alone. But if we are to be honest, we must include him, indeed, welcome him home.

Throughout the book, David Wojahn will return to the themes of distance and what is necessary to maintain the generous receptivity of the poet's mind. What is necessary, we find in the first section of this book, is necessary because Wojahn is a passionate man who deals with painful subjects: a mother crippled by polio ("The Astral Body"), a pathetic father lost to alcohol and daydreams nourished by a dull dead-end job ("Heaven for Railroad Men"), the death of a splendid poet whose work Wojahn loves ("Elegy for James Wright"), a blind grandmother ("Glaucoma"). The distance Wojahn aspires to might be called the innocent cooling of words. To deal with emotion, Wojahn must exercise adult control of language, yet keep alive his innocent and generous childlike receptivity to words. Wojahn feels obligated to include the total self in his writing though he knows that during the act of writing the distance between selves (workman and poet) must be maintained.

Keeping that distance can have sad consequences. "Border-Town Evening," the opening poem of the second section of the book, explores the emptiness of some lives; a butcher just off work sees

> . . . himself in the glass,
> one hundred yards from a foreign country,

and

> . . . wants
> to touch the face of the man there,
> who so resembles him in this light.

But unlike Wojahn who creates an admirable distance in order to cross it, the butcher "turns away toward home."

In the poem nothing is completed to satisfaction except the poem itself. To Wojahn the inability to welcome and "touch" that other self leads to a life of dissatisfaction. Like the poet he loves, James Wright, he will not exclude from his art that which by nature is unartistic. The crude and gross parts of the self belong too, and the poem created is their home as well, even if they had to be segregated from the aesthetic self during the poem's construction. It is to Wojahn's credit that he is too sophisticated to write the easy, painless poem. He pays the necessarily complicated personal price for his words.

Our obsessions ignore relative dramatic values. What grips mind and heart over and over may be far less dramatic as memory than experiences that initially shocked us. That too makes writing difficult: the poet can't depend on the material to carry the poem. In "Somewhere a Row of Houses," a man can't sleep not because of a childhood shock, but because he remembers that

> . . . somewhere there's a row of houses
> that won't let you rest, red brick, all identical.

> Delivering papers, you found a man on the steps
> in the snow, a screwdriver lodged in his chest.
> You can't say fear takes you over again, . . .
> . . . You're alone
> in familiar surroundings, and this
> is how the world intrudes, perfect rows.

Order can be more maddening than the bizarre. Wojahn doesn't question; he just accepts. But in that acceptance mysteriously lies Wojahn's opportunity to move us. At its best, language is passion, but as Valéry noted, the object of a poem is to excite passion in the reader. "The Precincts of Moonlight" excites me in that way, as do other poems in this volume. "Precincts" is one of the most compassionate and affecting poems I've seen written about a mentally handicapped person;

and I suspect that in addition to James Wright, Wojahn has read more than a little of Philip Levine and William Stafford. In style Wojahn more resembles Levine but in stance he seems closer to Stafford. He shows little hostility toward an unjust world, and he does not try to escape " . . . the fever and the vision we must live" ("Allegory: Attic and Fever").

The third section opens with "The Inside," which explores the love-hate relationship Wojahn has with his inner life.

> I hate the inner life . . .
> I'm tired of the thoughts I steer by.
> This is the inside, where stars
> keep revolving, revolving.

What artist doesn't feel this way about his art at times? And what artist doesn't go back to it, driven, and present it all over again.

If one thinks of originality as that which results in the brand new, then we can say that Wojahn is indifferent to originality. But if we accept the notion that originality means pertaining to origins, then Wojahn is a true original, living where " . . . only / the dead are breathing, their hands cupped gently / to whisper, again, their names into our ears" ("Buddy Holly").

In "Ice-Mist" Wojahn returns to his sad father.

> . . . He stands to breathe
> the ice-mist he's just expelled,
> his life so close he can't touch it.

His father's problems are similar to his own. Yet the father can't create that distance necessary to receive or "touch" his own life, while Wojahn can.

> And we learn sometimes to accept our breath,
> calm and pale as milk in snow:
> I'm standing at the window
> where I'm always made to stand,
> where this life is sometimes my own.

Where Wojahn's life is his own, that's where he finds his poems. At the risk of putting undue pressure on him (but I'm fatalistic about writing—nothing will stop Wojahn for long), he is already entering the company of Wright, Levine, and Stafford. It's an icehouse Wojahn has created, a cold place where he can turn on his warm lights of welcome.

Richard Hugo

I

Distance

Tonight the workmen
with red bandanas are building
a house across the street.
Light spills from the holes
they've left for windows.
They've inched across the roofbeams,
buckets of shingles in their arms.
This last man leans after
everyone's gone, his head
on a door that's propped on a tree.
I hear him singing to himself.

We both can't sleep—
his singing, and his hand
that drums a hammer again
and again into the ground.
The cats on the roof disturb him;
he stares and hammers,
hears me typing, or finds me
through the window, bent
to my lamp. I've come to admire

the distance between us,
the noises we make to ourselves
in the night, tired
as the lovers in a Japanese print
who've turned and wiped their genitals
with the blue silk scarves
they had stuffed in their mouths
while coupling.

The Astral Body

My handwriting's big, like grazing cattle.
I'm learning cursive on the dock
the summer that polio twists my mother's legs.
I write as she reads me the fable
of the prince who was sleepless for 100 years:
there's always a broken heart,
and I know sleepless nights are already a spell.

White gauze, the curtains too are a spell.
I wake. By a yellow bulb Aunt Hope and Mother
play cards on the porch all evening.
I look out on the lake where the misty
undead skim the water by moonlight.
The face at the window is only a branch
though it's breathing and calling my name.

Aunt Hope says we'll enter the astral body.
We'll give off light and be crippled
by light. The prince who is sleepless
will rise into light. My aunt lifts Mother
up from the table, darkens the lamp.
They stare at the water that hurts
as it shimmers. The astral body is also pain,

all pulsation and memory. It is not dark wood
or a walnut door, it is not a staircase
my mother won't climb. Mother, when you're nothing
but starlight that drills through the curtains,
when you're mist I can slice with my hands,
I'll wake like this, want to rise up,
cold, touching the light you've become.

Heaven for Railroad Men

You're still a young man,
he says, not to his son,
it's his bitterness he's
talking to and
at the restaurant
he orders a fourth round
before dinner.
With Mother wiping
her glasses at the table,

I help him from his chair
to the john. He pees slowly,
fingers like hams
on his fly, a complex
test of logic
for a man this drunk.
I'm splashing cold water in his face

and he tells me he's dying,
Don't say a thing to your Mother,
and please, Dave,
don't ever remember me like this.

I remember how you said you
needed to ride
the baggage cars forever,
passing prairie towns
where silos squat like
pepper shakers on dry earth.
I want to be six again
and sway with you

down the sagging rails
to Minot, Winnipeg, and beyond,
your mailsacks piled
like foothills of the Rockies.

You're unloading your government Colt,
unzipping your suitcase
for Canadian inspectors.
Father, when I touched you
I was trembling.

Heaven for railroad men
begins with a collapsed trestle.
The engine goes steaming
off into nothing.
There are no rails to hold you.
You're singing country-western
at the top of your lungs.
You go flying forever,
the door pulled open,
mailsacks scattered
into space like seed.

Eclipse

for my grandmother

Sudden evening. The light falters
as it did once on a lake

when you were a girl, forms
a wandering pattern on the water,

asymmetrical, like the body
of a one-celled animal

you saw that year through an eyepiece,
swimming, encased in cider vinegar.

Long ago. Light going out
on rushes and oak, or some creature

too insignificant to name.
What remains is a landscape

personal and foreign. You participate,
the three shapes in a rowboat

ripple out to the sudden dark:
your father and sister and you,

a child who raises a photo negative
to view the sun's obstruction.

Everything stills. Geese by the inlet
scud across the water to sleep

for it must be evening now,
last light, the moment when you learn

to fathom the eye's confusion,
the coming of change and time.

Obscurity. The stars come out.
So this is who you are,

your own eye gazing inward,
the light turned back, unwavering.

Wine

"like cups of wine thrown back into the bottle"
—James Moore

1

Midnight
and the pipes knock,
the language of steam.
George has played his flute
all night in the living room,
short pieces, stopping abruptly,
beginning again and again
in search of the right note.
Now he is a child wading into a lake,
learning to swim underwater
in the light the sun brings
to the sand on the lakebed.
I watch him scoop up handfuls of sand
and stone in the blurred green water,
holding them to his face,
just learning to see.

2

Today was the shortest day of the year.
I slept through the afternoon,
waking to lamplight,
to plants watered after sundown.
Outside the neighbors
try to rouse their cars.
Ignitions grind and howl.
The engines complain,
led aimlessly into darkness.
I drink wine straight from the bottle,

and I'm already drunk when my father phones,
talking of the job that's no good,
the money that's gone,
the spine that sways like a willow tree.
He would weep if he could.
They want to put me in traction,
give me a back brace
for a year and a half.
Who is this stranger who asks me for nothing?

3

I want to talk and,
Father, what can I say?
The winter nights are dark red.
We begin to live underwater
in small rooms
filled with flutesong,
the shades pulled down.
We cannot let go of this darkness.
We sit inside it, touch its walls,
like wine poured back into the bottle.
We write at midnight
with music in our rooms,
calling our fathers in the black evening.

4

Tonight I am wine.
My father is wine.
The glass sits on the table, full,
with no one to drink it.
This afternoon I dreamt
my father was running to meet me
and slipped on the ice
into a hole in the lake.

The scene kept repeating itself,
and I never reached him in time.
A thick film clouded his face
like the eyes of my grandfather
who died blind, whose last words
were *white, it's white*.

Now I swim down
to meet my father in the water,
cupping his temples in my hands.
He is crying into my palms,
and I can't yet see his face.

The Stories Behind Them

In 1957, Mother pulls back
the lime green strap of her swimsuit,
telling Father not to stand in the boat.
She pivots on the dock with the camera,
and again the shot will be blurred.

But his boat giving form to the water,
that's what I'll remember, the prow
cutting its momentary furrow
like a hand on my forehead in sleep.
I've had this fever for weeks
and can't leave my bed at the window.

I want to know what they're saying
as they point to the island,
the harbor lights just blinking on.
Do you know it's my face in the distance
through the curtains that bandage my eyes?
Father's displaying the evening's catch.
I'm asking for the sizes, the weights,
the stories behind them. But there's silence

as I whisper their names. Mother,
Father, I'm so tired and must let
the story grow simple, if I can: a woman
covered to her waist in water, a man
on a dock with a knife at sunset,
a hand that struggles with the insides of fish.

Elegy for James Wright

Now there's no returning
to sullen Ohio or Minnesota; now the pairs
of salt and pepper Indian ponies
grazing April fields
by Milbank on the South Dakota border,
their delicate spring coats ashimmer,
do not and never will exist.

And it's raining so pitifully
you'll never find them. Here,
an hour's drive to Mexico,
there's no such event as spring.
All night clouds have gathered
and what there is of April rain
needles the granulated riverbeds.

And who'd go back to Minnesota?
Is there any field where those horses
all the summer could graze,
almost human the way its grasses breathe?

I think if you were here you'd tell me.

I remember drinking
all afternoon with Peter
in St. Paul on the Fourth of July,
that summer we wrote *dark* in notebooks,
wrote *beautiful*, in poems that wanted
to sound like you,
and we drove down the highway

barely able to steer
to Rochester, Minnesota,
to find the ponies who blessed you.

My god, I believe we did it,
a herd of maybe twenty,
bodies rippling like smoke.
Gently we inched the singing
electric fence to greet them.
Yes, they came gladly
from a stand of pines to meet us,
luminous planets in the rain.
I wanted to lie down
right there forever in the saw grass,
among those cantering satellites.
I thought then I would never
again be afraid of dying.

Glaucoma

1

There's an olive grove inside the fence
that circles the home for the blind.
I drive each day past the gate
where they come to the crosswalk
in mismatched couples,
having one great thing in common.
I'm braked, the motor off,
making up names.
There's sightless Elena leaning
on the stoplight, twelve-year-old Samuel
gripping her wrist. Redhead Anya
drops her cane to the curb,
stops the traffic as she searches.
I always picture their dorms at night.
Roommates, Anya and Elena
drink wine after lights-out.
The gray, forbidden cat
nudges their knees for food.
Elena pours too much milk,
filling the bowl from fingertip to knuckle.

2

At first the drops sting.
The nurse holds my pulse and offers me gum.
This is the third test
in a month, various lenses.
I watch the doctor's forehead underwater:
G P X R. I have to correct myself twice.

Glaucoma, pressure on the retina's
subtle nerves; some,
like my grandmother, go crazy from it,
more than blind. I can't concentrate—
I'm five again at midnight,
wake to grandmother carrying blankets
to my bed. In the morning,
I'll stare at smudges her hands
have made for years along the walls,
see her turn from the dress pattern
laid out clumsy on the table,
her mouth full of pins. . . .

3

After bourbon all night,
we undress with the lights on,
do it in front of the closet mirror.
You're on top with eyes halfclosed
when I ask you to look at my face,
grab my neck and look
at my face. Your back's arched
forward, hair across my chest.
The first warm night this winter,
we open windows to the lights
in the valley. No one should be
permitted to love the moon, you say.
And each night it's smaller for me.
Even tonight, full.

4

I wake from the dream
where grandmother leads me
along the walls of an endless house,
stucco cutting our palms.

I sit up, touch
your sleeping face, try
to imagine blindness. One hand
across my eyes, the other
on the oranges, the wicker basket.
Still life in darkness. Oranges:
dwarf stars colliding. In the valley,
Elena's asleep in her chair.
Anya wraps her arms
around the cat. She's decided
his eyes are green, his fur
is brown and streaked with silver.

II

Border-Town Evening

The shops are closing now.
A street lamp's haze has settled on the doors
and a side of beef is noosed in a window
like a red moon about to set.
The butcher removes his apron,
pulling shades, turning the knob
as gently as a lover might.
The apron's folded under his arm
and drips a trail as he strolls down the walk

past the man with a cart
of orange canaries in wooden cages,
who's drunk and singing to his birds.
The birds are asleep
and he covers their cages with cloth.
An old song weaves
its needles through the butcher's mind.
He doesn't bother to remember the words.

Facing the leather-goods window,
he's come to himself in the glass,
one hundred yards from a foreign country,
breathing hard in the heavy altitude.
It's the moment when he wants
to touch the face of the man there,
who so resembles him in this light.
But he turns away toward home.
Bulbs shine down on the tables of the cantina
and last light is crossing the border.

Miracles

for Mary Logue

1

You phoned from Minnesota
when your sister died:
murdered by a stranger in her bed.
Your father two days later
found her body, and long distance
there was little I could say.
I thought of how I'd watched sometimes
my body from the ceiling as it slept,
but knew that I'd return
to wake, stare as the room
would shudder into view,
and I would join myself again.
Later with Steve you came to visit
and after *Picnic at Hanging Rock*,
a film both lovely and unbearable—
where the dead do not simply die
but disappear and somehow endure—
we heard you walk through the house
near dawn, all night unable to sleep.

2

In Mexico next day we ate and drank
at a restaurant in a cave, *turistas*
overlooking the border fence.
In the mission of San Xavier del Bac
the saints have wooden bodies.
The faithful bring them candles
and silver charms

no larger than a fingernail—
miracles—parts of the body
they pray will soon be cured:
hands and Egyptian eyes, cartoon feet,
heads in profile for the comatose,
so they will wake again,
leave the blue vaults of heaven
and come home. The raiments of the saint
pinned with them like burrs or constellations,
the immensity of loss
on the smallest imaginable scale.
The man in the shop took an interest in us
and showed us a bag of thousands:
cows and sheep and children,
even a crude, eight-pointed star.
Feeling foolish, we carried dozens
in a paper sack across the border.

3

Driving home that night I remembered
how you and I had lived one summer
in the borrowed house on the Mississippi,
took our meals on the terrace,
just oranges and cheese. And the woman
next door who'd always wave,
watering ferns and nasturtiums.
She would tell us about Poland
and the war, how in time even Poland
became consoling. Since memory becomes revision,
like sentiment in foolish songs,
we smooth our pasts and loss
until they're simple, ignore the fights
she had with her son, and evenings
she'd visit us drunk and weeping.

The night we called the ambulance for her—
the medics with their doubled
fists upon her chest—
I wanted to remember her serene,
though her face was blue with pain.
She asked you to hurry next door
for her medal of Saint Christopher,
some Polish inscription she read
out loud to no one, tight
Cyrillic letters on the back.

4

And Mary, what we bring from the dead
is small, memory and gesture,
the way someone looked during a picnic once,
holding a black and yellow moth
by the tips of its wings to show you,
her hair obscuring her eyes;
like the star Ancharion Ten
in the constellation of the swan,
dead tonight over twenty years,
so there is no light
at the end of its beam we see,
only its darkness, compressed and final.
I would like us to walk
out of our hearts, under the looming
abundant sky. I would like us to pray,
and you and I can stand all night
and search the sky for the dead
who are larger now than ever thought,
more distant and enduring.
And we are the source
of what shines down.

Noon: On the Death of Cesare Pavese, Turin, 1950

This could be a photograph: you by the barbershop
at noon beside the blind accordion player.
He touches his pimpled face between songs.
You've turned to see your small pale body in the window,
a distorted reflection in the spiraling pole.
You don't want your breath to cloud the glass.
All the doors are open in the heat,
and here a cat's eyes blaze out from inside.
They remind you of a six-year-old child
opening his father's toilet kit in secret,
smelling menthol, and running his hand
along the stinging edge of a razor.
Your father's pipe was like the ones
the hairy chested workmen smoke by the hotel,
big men you envy. Beneath the ceiling fan,
the bored desk clerk reads *L'Osservatore*
for the second time. The last thing you do
is ask him to bring up a phone. No,
the last thing you do is hold your ringing temple
where you've shot yourself,
upsetting the washstand when you fall.

Your solitude, you wrote,
would be simple and weightless,
curling like heat-haze from the rooftops.
But the sun has not set in twenty-eight years.
It's noon still in Turin
and I can only ask if you're happy like this,
mouth gaping at the sun
that shines through the fraying curtains.

Below the hotel, a toothless woman holds
the accordion player's hand to tell his fortune.
Once, she might have predicted
fame for you, but you're still dead
after all these years. Aren't you tired yet?
Your solitude must be heavy now, complex,
like a page from a book in a language
no one would read: a battered copy
of *Das Kapital,* open on the floor of an attic
with your small handwriting in the margins.

Floating Houses

The night mist leaves us yearning for a new location
to things impossibly stationary,
the way they'd once float houses
made from dismantled ships, brass and timber,
from Plymouth, Massachusetts, across the sound
to White Horse Beach. You were only a boy.

Years later, gazing out to the red buoys
of the harbor, you sought those houses, each the location
of your childhood's end. Jon, I make this all sound
too complex. Our view of time is stationary,
a long prediction of remorse. We're drinking in timber,
camping above Tucson, Arizona. Below, the houses

are vague points of light, describing a grief you've housed
since watching those buildings careen on water, a boy
too sullen for your father. So the aspens creak like timber
in an aging sloop. The others sleep. You locate
the figure of your son, small and stationary,
but tell me he'll die young, body unsound,

a childhood diabetic. The bourbon makes you sound
entranced—to think one day you'll return to the house
to find that you've outlived him, maybe the radio station
playing some popular song. Outliving the boy,
you'll outlive yourself. Drunk, we've lost our location.
I shine my flashlight to find the others. The timbre

of your voice grows slack. Leaves and timber
rustle in the promise of rain, in the sound
of distant thunder that, like death, has no location.
Below, relentless clouds will cover houses.
The campfire sputters, then grows, buoyed
by wind, our bodies the only things stationary.

Because of death, our small, unstationary
lives become narration—a child is lost in timber
in a fable when night approaches. The boy
can't even see his hands. Only owl-cry, the sound
of his heart. But soon the aspens part, the houses
of his village appear, their location

precise and consoling. He's stationary, not a sound
from below. Beyond the timber, floating houses.
And there his papa's lantern, a light the boy can locate.

Somewhere a Row of Houses

for Bill Olsen

Already what I've told you isn't enough.
Plenty of moonlight, the plane came in low
and your car was pinned in the T of its shadow.
So you traveled a minute, car in shade, plane gliding.
That was all. He swooped up to clouds, the foothills.
You understood: calmness is provisional,
a hand on your forehead in sleep, or the apartment
just as you left it, still locked, the trembling windows.

If only we'd discover nothing more about ourselves,
though our mornings stay sardonic, and nights
go on as usual. So you stare at the light bulb's
dimming orange filament, then adjust your eyes
until sleep is a task you were meant for,
though you still hear a siren blocks away
and somewhere there's a row of houses
that won't let you rest, red brick, all identical.

Delivering papers, you found a man on the steps
in the snow, a screwdriver lodged in his chest.
You can't say fear takes you over again, or the thought
of his hand, gripping a bottle and glove.
It's not enough to say you've been drinking all night
and now the room is spinning. You're alone
in familiar surroundings, and this
is how the world intrudes, perfect rows.

The Precincts of Moonlight

Her first child belongs to the crows
and his days go circling the yellow-black fields

summers and into the falls. He scans
the horizon, mouth in a sticky O,

like a spirit caged to infinite space.
Winged One, she calls, *Winged One, come here.* Receding,

he pulls off his straw hat and waves, showing his tuft
of obsidian hair. He's not coming back just yet.

She remembers how crows are small black rivers
like stairways leading to rooms

that can't be rooms, only the hallways of space.
And then, how she watched him last night

in the ruined farmhouse across the road
where only a chimney and staircase are left

jutting up to the vacant precincts of moonlight.
He was stepping so lightly then,

who at sixteen forgets his own name, and shits himself
like the mindless, fear-mad prey of barn owls.

He belonged to the crows and stood
for hours on the stairway's precipice, weaving

a dance like crows in flight, until his brother,
with rope and fists, carried him struggling down.

Allegory: Attic and Fever

All day the fever tells lies.
The armchair vibrates with the train
from the yards below the window. The new snow
falls like moths on a soldier's collar,
like the long white dreams of those condemned.
They've moved great slabs of marble from the country
for building a new station in spring.
But now it's a huge icehouse from the window,
children climbing abandoned cranes and pulleys.

Fever is an allegory, like the tale I wrote
of the fire in the bookstore. No one wanted it,
as I don't want coal or bread. This morning,
bending down to look through the crack in the floorboards,
I watched Katya the whore undress her client—
a bald man in suspenders, stains on his shirtfront.
Her fraying garters, and his buttocks between them,
grunting forward. Finished, he took her towel
and wiped himself. Like me. Like me

erasing a page. It's not allegorical:
I begin again. This time, not a fire in a bookstore,
but the station house below me, burning.
And the train on fire pulling forward
across the trestle, lighting all Oslo
at midnight. The cries in the train are the beauty
of no escape, like a fever refusing to break.
I've a coal in my mouth, singing.
Hear it steaming in my mouth.

Let me tell you how the first snow comes
in the country of my dream. The lake's not frozen,
for the fever's in the water.
I'm in a glass bottomed rowboat, watching
the other world, the one below.
I'm King of Perch, Archduke of Cod.
But the fever's in the water and they die:
my hair falls out, all goes milky in snow.
But Katya's here, undressing me, telling me

how weary I am. No one would call her beautiful
or able to control her fate. I tell her this is not a dream,
but the fever and the vision we must live.

No Language We Know

1

A cobalt glaze surrounds the edge
of the earthen mug unevenly:
strange terrain like a map of Asia
where travelers still can lose themselves.
Beside me, the kerosene lamp
left on all night, the clear liquid spent.
I brush my hair in a triangular
fragment of mirror, as you pace back from the barn,

hands smeared. The blood and gristle
foams down the sink. Later,
I'll mop stains from the kitchen floor
as you sit heavy in your chair,
the radio still playing stations
from Nogales and beyond. No language we know,
the music pulsing in brittle waves.

I remember another summer. I was twelve,
sharing a room with my older sister.
I stood at the window to watch the sun twist down
or see a stranger kissing Marcy on the throat.
Sometimes he was bearded or Mexican.
At times they'd lie together by the olive grove.
I'd lose all but their cries in the growing dark.

By midnight, dry stalks in Marcy's hair.
I'd pick them out in the oil lamp's shimmer.
She'd sway half-dressed on the edge of the bed,
and I'd ease her head to the pillow.

2

The rain, which always frightens me,
sent me to myself, monsoon clouds drifting
like fists across the eastern range.
You called them *hammers of God.*
Today was the first time ever
I refused you my body. And now you sleep
in the radio's din. Never in my life
have I touched myself like this.
Sweat like fish scales glistens my forehead.

Rain still batters the tin roof.
God is wearing his cleated boots. He holds
a black obsidian knife and spreads
a long damp stain against the wall.
You didn't believe me when I talked of Him.

Each summer you'd pick a calf to hold alone
in a pen three weeks, feeding her milk
from a nippled bottle. This one would come
whenever you called. You gave her
several names: *Tania, Melissa, Vanessa.*
Today you opened her skull with a steel rod,
hung her upside down from a barn beam,
breaking her back legs with the noose.
Closing her eyes, you reached the jugular

on the third try, catching her blood
in buckets for sausage. The bladder,
as a joke, you filled balloonlike
and presented to me. You were wearing
my frayed kitchen apron, stiff and spotted umber.
My mug had shattered on the floor.

3

Always, with our nearest neighbor three miles off,
I'd insist you close the bedroom door
before sex or sleep. Once, when the wind
clapped it open, I started and turned away,
your pearl string of semen on my knee and thigh.
My tears that afternoon were for
something I could never tell you:

the wish to be silent and deliberate,
distant, like those fires
in the pines in the eastern mountains
we watched at sunset one August night.
It was then I knew you'd be propped in your chair
in this moment of final clarity,
asleep with a long red gash along your throat.

How could I tell you of this fire of mine
I've set free to burn such a long way off?
Part of me, but not *in* me. How
can I explain? It's this evening wind,
all sound and deepened color, like the flocks
of purple martins at my window as a child,
in the branches of the mulberry thick as hair.

They'd strip the tree clean of berries,
spreading their ink-blue droppings on the house.
They'd rush up in one huge gust,
in a turbulence outside themselves.

Portrait with Oranges

I know again tonight the face is made of halves,
one that hides itself repeatedly, one that turns
its sweater of flesh to the world. Her name
is Lisa. She's come to be painted,
the great-aunt's daughter in a wicker chair.
On the blue tile by the window. I want

nothing pretty about it. The face must be
this division of the world and self, or the point
at which they merge, like a hand
lifting a teacup and trembling. Sailboats:
she's watching one through the window.
The lake by a sliver of moon, almost evening.

What she sees are two moons, one that billows
like a lung, one that turns the sunset gray
when pinned to clouds. She tells me on the train today
she ate oranges the color of the fields
she passed, and in the window, swathed in light,
she met herself. So tonight she wants only

to be that couple on the lake. I'm the man,
fingers tangled in the rigging, unpinning her hair.
And she takes off her necklace when kissed.
She wants to be another, whose hands
are still as the light on tile—
even grace, the face's divisions

blurring into one, symmetrical as oranges
split by a knife. I pin up her hair,
stroke a neck as pale as light that's dying.

Now the light will tremble
like her hand without a ring,
holding an orange or poised at the throat.

Weldon Kees in Mexico, 1965

Evenings below my window
the sisters of the convent of Saint Teresa
carry brown jugs of water from a well
beyond a dry wash called *Mostrenco*.
Today it was hard to waken,
and I've been dead to the world ten years.
They tread the narrow footbridge
made of vines and planks, sandals clicking:
brown beads and white wooden crosses
between hands that are also brown.
Over the bridge they travel in a white-robed line
like innocent nurses to a field hospital.

Exactly ten. I've marked it on the calendar.
And Maria, who speaks no English,
is soaping her dark breasts by the washstand.
Yesterday she said
she'd like to be a painter and sketched,
on the back of a soiled napkin,
a rendition of a cholla
with her lipstick. She laughed,
then drew below each nipple
a smudged rose. Weldon

would have been repelled
and fascinated, but Weldon is dead.
I watched him fall to the waves
of the Bay, the twelfth suicide that summer.
He would have been fifty-one this year,
my age exactly, an aging man.

Still he would not be a fool
in a poor adobe house, unwinding
a spool of flypaper from a hook
above the head of his child bride.

When she asks my name, I tell her
I am Richard, a good midwestern sound.
She thinks Nebraska is a kingdom
near Peru, and I
the exiled Crown Prince of Omaha.
I've promised to buy her a box of paints
in a shop by my palace in Lincoln.
We'll go back, Maria and I,
with the little sisters of Saint Teresa
who are just now walking across the bridge
for water to be blessed at vespers.

III

The Inside

Because this is the moment
when stars grow ominously small,
there's room again for passivity.
There's no pale green flooding the bed—
the corner bar has shut off its sign,
and love isn't even disease anymore,
not even a secret we're
forever disclosing. As a child

I feared bridges and nuns.
They kept me awake, staring at Christ,
his arms pinned into the wall.
Worry is better now.
You sleep beside me until morning,
a habit we'll repeat
until we've had enough. The stars

must collapse within themselves to rest.
In the mirror I know age
is the face imploding.
I hate the inner life—you snore
with your back against me.
The artistry of sleeplessness
is a mind as heavy as a landscape of trains,
coils of a mountain road.
I'm tired of the thoughts I steer by.
This is the inside, where stars
keep revolving, revolving.

Matins

In the fog are streetlights I confuse with moons,
but soon the puddles from last night's rain

flame an instant, stare into themselves.
Across the street, the trashmen look

almost stately on the curb, examining
the crippled lawn chair. Without sleep all night

I've lain for hours in the breathless room,
reading an endless novel

of complication and deceit, of intrigues
the living cannot care about,

though they live them. For a moment,
I wanted to judge my life

without intensity, the way a minor character
enters a drawing room.

There's the graceless music of his accent
and his mornings are always difficult,

aimless like traffic noise. It's only slightly wrong,
how we choose to seek ourselves out of context.

Distorting the light, the stucco wants
to be abstract, the way a story wants

no ending, only a manner of telling.
So formless thunderclouds brought rain

from Baja and Kino Bay,
from towns I've forgotten the names for.

So fishermen there, vague outlines, are rising
to bail their vessels with coffee tins

until the sky is suddenly clear. So this man at dawn
shaves with his hand mirror facing the sun,

the beach harshly white,
his face, for a moment, in flames.

Ice-Mist

Minnesota winter, drained of color,
and the milk he delivered minutes ago
has frozen in its tray on the step.
My father leaves the truck to gaze
at pinnacled ice on Lake Superior.
Not yet dawn, it's 1946,
and the bottle he drops
abstractedly on the sidewalk
glows like a single rooming house lamp.
My father wants to know
if he can die, asking snow
and a woman he won't meet for years,
asking an unborn son.

Last night he walked
from the movies alone,
staring long at the yellow
marquees, parking-lot coupes in snow,
as if he could take
his life in his hands and shake it,
a glove, an overshoe. He stands to breathe
the ice-mist he's just expelled,
his life so close he can't touch it.

*

Last night December snow
in the desert foothills.
Near dawn I walked until
I lost myself, having no answer

to give you. By noon the snow
was gone. I came to myself again.
And in the story I've been telling
you rise and pull the crystals
of frozen milk from your overcoat.
You inch up the hill again,
truck in low and pushing hard
to a field where a snow fence
has bowed all night to the wind.
And we learn sometimes to accept our breath,
calm and pale as milk in snow:
I'm standing at the window
where I'm always made to stand,
where this life is sometimes my own.

Against the Windows

*"They all stretch out their hands to me:
but they are too far away!"*
—*Delmore Schwartz*

There's always some presentiment: the way a skylight
    inflicts the evening on the tiles of the dance pavilion
and the two Italian women take the floor, 1939,
    Bertolucci's *The Conformist*. I think of how
in two days' time the blonde woman will be dead,
    a hat and sable in the mountain snow, the blood
a formal arc around her. But all night
    the women seem to dance, and now the moon
has shattered through its black enclosure of trees
    like the bone china plate I once broke on a mirror,
destroying, for a second, my father's hard reflection.

A moment ago, the bedroom mirror, I saw myself
    at forty, fatherly and beardless, and the veins
on my forehead throbbed, not like rivers
    or crooked roads, only blue, elemental blood.
Like the oddity of light in a furnished room,
    the face is a big, foolish moon, and a figure in a stained
black overcoat collapses in New York on a hotel stairs.
    Groceries overturned, he clutches his failed heart.
It's summer, 1966, and for months he's reeled
    on liquor and pills. Afraid of infection and friends,
he's found wearing a surgeon's starched white mask.

I know how the face becomes a mask, afraid
    of others, afraid of death. It's not 1966,
not 1939, but late in the century, late in October,
    and I live next door to a convent house
with a woman and a life I can't describe.
    From the window I watch the sisters

of Saint Cecilia cover roses against the frost
or move in white shadows beyond their curtains.
They're married to Christ and the evening is cool.
We stare at each other against the windows.
The face itself must be transparent.

Buddy Holly

What there's been of winter moves away,
and after dawn it's warm again, another easy thing
to sentimentalize. I walked this morning with the dog
around a tiny, artificial lake,
among swans and eucalyptus, and read of Buddy Holly
in the Sunday *Globe*. Dead twenty years,
his shattered glasses from the plane crash rediscovered
in a county morgue locker in Clear Lake, Iowa.
We talked of this, Hank and I, over beers
and underdone chicken, and nights when he drinks

alone in his house, Hank plays Buddy Holly until dawn.
How much, he asked last night, would those glasses
be worth today? I told him thousands, thousands.
How much can we remove from the dead
for our private, selfish use? Buddy Holly died younger
than I am today. We dusted off the old LPs
and tried as best we could to mourn him.
He once said he wanted to come back
from the dead—he and his child bride—as swans.
Because they're beautiful. Because they're mates for life.

There's Hank's wife in the photo
before her death, before the unappeasable lingering.
Sammy in her arms in Boston. Hank's taught Sammy
to sing Buddy Holly, in a voice that makes you certain
he understands, to stand in a chair and hoot
and mime a perfect, electric guitar: moonlit dance pavilion,

the wind now hushed, the reverie of moments
when everything beyond the singer stills. And only
the dead are breathing, their hands cupped gently
to whisper, again, their names into our ears.

Above Palm Desert

Impossible to sink in the Salton Sea
though several drown
on the water each year like buoys,
and L.A. smog lies down on the shoreline
like mist in Victorian prints.
Campers and sparrows, a cookout grill.
Your father was talking
about Zeppo Marx,
last of the brothers to die,
who only had talent for investments
and women less than half his age.
This wasn't a place to camp at or linger.
Those kids in the distance
floated beer cans on the water and shot them.

So I read in the car about Europe,
the troubled fourteenth century,
the great cathedrals already built,
and the Hundred Years' War truly that long.
Saint Catherine of Avignon hired a scribe
for recording her daily
ecstatic trances. It's all there on paper,
arrows of Christ that pierced her.
Zeppo was found
face down in his Palm Springs Jacuzzi
the evening your father
talked endlessly of stocks,
argued ceaselessly with both of us.

The Salton Sea cannot support life.
St. Catherine of Avignon died of the plague,
and I drove to the mountains above Palm Desert
alone to watch the lights of the rich
glimmer below me like candles
a man six hundred years ago could write by.
He put down the visions
someone else said were flowing from God.
The words came thoughtlessly,
nothing his own to possess him.
Late and moonless: I wanted
to be like the rich, their minds
on money, their lights going slowly out.

Cold Glow: Icehouses

Because the light this morning is recondite
like figures behind curtains from a long way off,
because the morning is cold and this room is heatless,
I've gone without sleep, I brood.
The protocol of memory: the faucet dripping
into a sponge, then thinking of the way
I saw White Bear Lake freeze over
twenty years ago in Minnesota, the carp oblivious below.

I thought last night of Solomon Petrov,
a Ukrainian rabbi in my college science books
afflicted with total recall, a pathological memory
that made perspective impossible.
Once for doctors he *remembered* running for a train
in Petersburg in winter. They recorded
his quickened pulse, body temperature plunging.
The death by fever of his first wife Tania
was not remembered, but continually relived.

And memory is not accomplishment.
Last night again you described for me
our child pulled dead from your womb. In sleep you talked
to yourself and the child, who passed unnamed
wholly into memory. Now you wanted peace,
some distance. And every memory, said Solomon Petrov,
must proceed unchanged in the mind, going on
like smoke to designate itself again
like a second floor window where I stood as a boy
to watch the fishermen park their cars
on the lake, icehouse lights in the evening below.

Or our child whose name is only ash,
is only a thought too hurtful to free.
Mornings like these, he floats at the window, waiting
and mouthing his name, there through a tangent of ice,
his face and hands ashimmer.

The Man Who Knew Too Much

I've finished with the listlessness
of snow on pine boughs, or the page's invitations,
also snow. That's why this morning
the pines shake it off in gusts,
why I'm tired of the ways we look at ourselves.
From the window I watch you
throwing pinecones for the dogs,
resin on your glove, their breath that rises
like the drastic lights of a winter city
and illustrates nothing. Before,
I thought our lives, these mornings,
could all be ennobling and abstract
but the sky has whitened for days—
there are more than six sides to every question.

Last night you brushed your hair
a hundred strokes in the TV's light
that flickered thirties movies until dawn:
Hitchcock's *The Man Who Knew Too Much*,
who saved himself through irony
and fear. All these mazes of plot—
I can't let them go, as after those nights
we'd argue for hours, finally seeing
we'd come to nothing. We lived in a neighborhood
of Blacks and Chicanos and I'd walk away
to the Mexican movies, though I'd lost
my Spanish years before. This is the way
it always seemed: someone talks and you know
you won't understand. The hombre puts a pheasant
on the kitchen table. The mujer begins to weep.

Abstract movement, where some feeling is trapped
like the hombre frowning at a steamed-up mirror.
He cleans it and forgets what he was thinking.
And I'm leaving my seat, weary
of the dialogue, tired enough for home.

Patagonia Gorge

The road edged down
to a canyon that's been made
an artificial lake,

large enough for rowboats and canoes,
with an island like a floating retina,
scrub oak and cactus, a refuge

for egrets and cranes.
They made their heavy arcs on the water,
coming to rest in skeletal branches.

You stayed up late
another night. Hours before dawn
I left you sleeping

and found on the island
the bones of a crane, the vertebrae
an abacus in sand.

The delicate skull
I put in my rucksack and remembered
the journals of Audubon,

who'd fill the hammerlock with powder,
shoot his birds to draw them.
Musket shot, the crane veers down

like a child's kite,
then a figure in a birch canoe
with chamois dries the feathers.

On shore he draws it, imagining flight,
shading majestic, lovingly detailed.
I thought of our child who will not be born,

yolk of color you carried and lost,
just the eye of a crane,
open and staring.

I still can't distinguish
refusal from loss. Once Audubon found
the nest of the crane, fat chalky eggs

buried in down, and opened the shell
to draw the unborn bird, its pin-sized beak,
wings already straining.

Another Coast

The woman singing in the house
next door draws her bath,
a country-western song—
someone's heart is broken in El Paso—
then she pulls the shades.
We've never spoken, but nights
I watch her set the table for her lover
who visits weekends and outside filets
the bluefish he's just caught.
Later, they'll tip glasses on
the balcony. Animated talk,
then such composure on their faces.

Pointless now to say
how things should have been better with us.
The way I miss you makes the days
portentous, trees not simply barren,
and I walk the tapered
streets of this seaside town,
inns all shuttered, faltering shingles.

Yesterday, a bottle-nosed dolphin
beached herself beyond the pier
and lived for hours. The cafe waiters
checkered her with tablecloths
they'd dipped in seawater
to keep her damp and breathing.
A crowd had gathered
and the next-door couple with their shiny Nikon
argued loudly about who should take the picture.

Years ago, another coast,
we fought all evening in the small apartment,
finally sleeping in separate corners.
Several times we woke, not thinking
there was more to say and later stood
a long time at the window
to watch the taverns' blurry neons—
mugs and dancing glasses—
going out in sequence before the dark,
where a man and woman stood
to batter each other haplessly,
breaking bottles on the street
but not upon themselves.
Maybe some bruises, a little blood.
Finished, they embraced
and parted, the woman shouting *call me,*

call me when you get up.

Flour

Because her hands are freckled
she's rubbed them with a special cream,
waking early on Thanksgiving morning,
1955. My mother polishes
her mother's silver. Tired
or bored, she gives the chamois cloth to me.
Outside, the sky arranges itself for snow

as my father, on the road in Spearfish,
leans from the baggage car door
to catch a single flake in his glove.
He knows the train will follow snow
all day east to Minneapolis, viscous ice
already on the rivers.
And when he bends to his thermos,
feet propped on a stranger's coffin
bound express for Fond du Lac,
twenty-five years have passed

and I wake in a room in Massachusetts
to scan the low tide ice
beyond my window. Mornings like these
I can't complete my parents' faces
or my own—father dozing
between Alexandria and Fergus Falls,
mother in her mother's scarf,
setting out sumac for sparrows.
Mornings like these, I'm five again
and waving at the window
to her figure in the snow,

a moment so composed
I'll want it back, my breath
an almost perfect circle.

*

In all his work
there is only one window
and a single room. Only
the clean-swept tiles of a bourgeois house.
But also, says Proust of Vermeer,
our lives are ennobled
as heightened gestures of perspective.
The face and hands
of the maiden pouring milk,
the wall map of Europe
with its compass points—
clouds with human faces—
all this is reflected
in the lustre of a copper bowl
in the blonde girl's languid hands,
timeless in light,
the distance captivated.
This is the grand deception,
that the painter holds us here,
the world he denies us
immense and perfectly arranged.
My painter friend
said Vermeer made her weep
for what she couldn't have.

*

All afternoon, the first November snow
had clarified the fields,
roads disengaged
from trees and houses.
By evening, only stillness.
As I walked, I came back to myself,
the single gesture the landscape made,
continually shifting—
as if I could glimpse
from the corner of my eye,
my father turning endlessly
the red lid of the thermos, mother
in her mother's scarf
setting out sumac for sparrows,
arthritic Vermeer as he lifts
his daughter's wrist to pose.

I wanted to tell you
I was comforted by this.
In 1955, I grew lost
in the winter forest beyond our house.
Only snowlight, late evening.
Stepping free of the elms
to the vista of home, the porch light
and mother calling, was a way of seeing
my life diminish
to a landscape of blurred particulars.

I might now tell you
I was tranquil then, a self
beyond conception. Mother
had been baking, mother in the doorway
and its wedge of light,
dusted to her elbows with flour,
bending to cup my face
in her hands, delicately whitening
the cheek and forehead of her son.

Climbing Down

for Mick Fedullo

Our game today
was finding the oddest stone.
Mine was the etched

twin of my finger, yours
a pumice globe. We walked
the fissures of the sand wash

until dark, like the children
we were in our stories,
how we each had a tree fort

to hide in toward evening.
Our mothers' voices broke
with our names. We kept still:

so this, we thought,
is what it means to be dead.
But soon came the fear

of being forgotten or remembered
imprecisely. Climbing down,
we told them they were not

our real mothers, but sleep
was easy then,
like the noise of wind

through porch screens.
I want to talk now
about nothing self-conscious:

the red blooms of cactus,
the unwashed plates, the cat
with a spider in her mouth.

But we come to ourselves,
climbing down, or bending
to a stone, moments

we learn to rest within our faces
the way the Aztec dead
in masks of stone and onyx,

who were strapped to trees
with broken arms and legs,
could never haunt the living.

And they would hear the wind forever,
its rise and fall,
like the first time we noticed our breathing.

Notes and Acknowledgments

Lines 4 and 5 of "Distance" are adapted from William Arrowsmith's translation of Cesare Pavese's poem "Houses Under Construction." My poem on Pavese does not necessarily reflect the actual circumstances of his suicide.

"Weldon Kees in Mexico, 1965": Although Kees apparently jumped from the Golden Gate Bridge in 1955, his body was never found.

The rabbi in stanzas 2 and 3 of "Cold Glow: Icehouses" is loosely based on the subject of A. L. Luria's *The Mind of a Mnemonist: A Study in Memory Pathology*.

Lines 26–28 of "The Man Who Knew Too Much" are adapted from a poem by Philip Dacey.

"Elegy for James Wright" is for Peter Mladinic. "Buddy Holly" is for Henry Combellick.

I am indebted to Jon Anderson and, especially, to the late James L. White for their encouragement and assistance. I would also like to thank the Fine Arts Work Center in Provincetown and the Corporation of Yaddo for fellowships which enabled me to complete this book.

Acknowledgment is made to the following publications for poems which originally appeared in them:

The American Poetry Review: "Flour"
Black Warrior Review: "Patagonia Gorge"
Blue Moon News: "No Language We Know"
Columbia: "Weldon Kees in Mexico, 1965"
Crazy Horse: "Portrait with Oranges"
Cutbank: "Heaven for Railroad Men"
Dacotah Territory: "Wine"
Gilt Edge: "Ice-Mist"
The Iowa Review: "Distance"
Ironwood: "Glaucoma"
The Missouri Review: "Climbing Down"
The New Yorker: "The Man Who Knew Too Much"
The North American Review: "Cold Glow: Icehouses"
Poetry: "Elegy for James Wright," "Miracles," "Matins"
Poetry East: "Noon: On the Death of Cesare Pavese, Turin, 1950"
Poetry Now: "The Stories Behind Them"
Ploughshares: "The Astral Body"
Quarterly West: "Border Town Evening"
raccoon: "Somewhere a Row of Houses," "Buddy Holly"
Salmagundi: "Allegory: Attic and Fever"
Shankpainter: "Against the Windows," "Above Palm Desert"
Whetstone: "The Precincts of Moonlight"

"Weldon Kees in Mexico, 1965" was reprinted in *The Pushcart Prize VI: Best of the Small Presses,* Pushcart Press/Avon Books, 1981; "Heaven for Railroad Men" was reprinted in the anthology *Brother Songs,* Holy Cow Press, 1979; "Distance" was reprinted in the *Anthology of College Prizewinners* (selections by Stanley Kunitz), Academy of American Poets, 1980; "Cold Glow: Icehouses" was reprinted in the *Anthology of Magazine Verse and Yearbook of American Poetry,* 1981.